GI

M000309076

The colourful Georgian Doors of Dublin are now an integral part of any tourist's visit to the Capital. These brightly painted doors, many of which are situated around the Fitzwilliam and Merrion Square areas of Dublin, give to the City a character that is unique throughout the World.

This book features thirty of these doors taken from the REAL IRELAND poster, DOORS OF DUBLIN.

Brian Murphy

Little Books of Ireland

First Published by
REAL IRELAND DESIGN LIMITED
27 Beechwood Close, Boghall Road, Bray Co.
Wicklow, Ireland.
Tel: (01) 2860799. Fax: (01) 2829962.
1993 1999

Design and Layout: Brian Murphy.
Photography © Liam Blake.

ISBN 0946887608

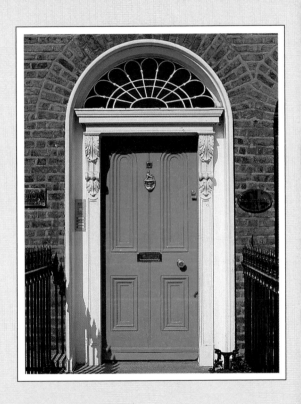